THE COMPLETE BOOK OF
HANDWRITING
GRADES K-3

AMERICAN
EDUCATION
PUBLISHING™

An imprint of Carson-Dellosa Publishing LLC
Greensboro, North Carolina

American Education Publishing™
An imprint of Carson-Dellosa Publishing LLC
P.O. Box 35665
Greensboro, NC 27425 USA

ISBN 0-7696-8558-7
Printed in the USA

07-110151151

Table of Contents

Let's Warm Up! 4–9

Manuscript Handwriting

Letter Practice 10–113
Numbers 114–118
Shape Words 119
Color Words 120–122
Days of the Week 123–127
Months of the Year 128–132
Seasons 133
Weather Words 134–135
Holidays 136–137
School Words 138–143
School Tools 144
Praise Words 145
Safety Words 146–147
Family Words 148–151
Neighborhood Words 152–154
Place Words 155–156
Food Words 157–159
Direction Words 160–161
Sports Words 162–165
Money Words 166–168
Action Words 169–170
Adjectives 171
Comparison Adjectives 172–177
"Writing a Letter" Words 178
Thank-You Note 179
Friendly Letter 180
Envelope 181

Cursive Handwriting

Letter Practice 182–285
Numbers 286–289
Shape Words 290
Color Words 291–293
Days of the Week 294–297
Months of the Year 298–302
Seasons 303
Weather Words 304
Holidays 305–306
School Words 307–310
School Tools 311
Safety Words 312
Family Words 313–316
Neighborhood Words 317–319
Money Words 320–322
Action Words 323–324
Adjectives 325
Comparison Adjectives 326–331
"Writing a Letter" Words 332
Thank-You Note 333
Friendly Letter 334
Spelling Words 335
Pronouns 336–337
Contractions 338
Language Arts Words 339–340
Literature Words 341–342
Math Words 343–348
Science Words 349
Art Words 350
Music Words 351–352

Let's Warm Up!

Practice by tracing the lines.

Name _____

Practice by tracing the lines.

Name _____

Practice by tracing the lines.

Name _____

Practice by tracing the lines.

Name _____

Practice by tracing the lines.

Name _____

Practice by tracing the lines.

Name _____

Aa

Practice by tracing the letter.
Then write the letter.

Name _____

A A A A A A A A A A

a a a a a a a

Practice by tracing the words.
Then write the words.

Name _____

Aa

alligator

apple

ant

Alaska

11

Aa

Alligators and ants

eat apples

Write the sentence. Name _____

Alligators and ants
eat apples.

Bb

Practice by tracing the letter.
Then write the letter.

Name _____

B B B B B B B

b b b b b b b

Practice by tracing the words.
Then write the words.

Name _____

Bb

bear

ball

bee

Bobby

15

Write the phrase.

Name _____

Brave Bobby

baseball bat

Write the sentence. Name _____

Brave Bobby buys a
baseball bat.

Cc

Practice by tracing the letter.
Then write the letter.

Name _____

C C C C C C C C

c c c c c c c

Practice by tracing the words.
Then write the words.

Name _____

cats

cookies

cards

Chuck

Cc

Name _____

cool cats

play cards

Write the sentence.

Name _____

Cc

Cool cats play cards.

Dd

Practice by tracing the letter.
Then write the letter.

Name _____

Practice by tracing the words.
Then write the words.

Name _____

duck

dog

dance

Danny

Dd

Name _____

Danny dances

dandy dog

Write the sentence.

Name _____

Danny dances with a

dandy dog.

Ee

Practice by tracing the letter.
Then write the letter.

Name _____

Practice by tracing the words.
Then write the words.

Name _____

elephant

egg

elbow

Ellie

Ee

Write the phrase.

Every evening

Ellie eats

Write the sentence.

Name _____

Every evening Ellie eats

eggs.

Ff

Practice by tracing the letter.
Then write the letter.

Name _____

Practice by tracing the words.
Then write the words.

Name _____

frog

fish

fox

Florida

Ff

Write the phrase.

Name _____

Four foxes

Five fish

Write the sentence.

Name _____

Four foxes and five fish fly to Florida.

Practice by tracing the letter.
Then write the letter.

Name _____

G G G G G G G G

g g g g g g g

Practice by tracing the words.
Then write the words.

Name _____

giraffe

grass

glasses

Gretchen

Gretchen wears

gray glasses

Write the sentence. Name _____

Gretchen wears gray glasses.

Hh

Practice by tracing the letter.
Then write the letter.

Name _____

Practice by tracing the words.
Then write the words.

Name _____

hippo

hat

heart

Hannah

Write the phrase.

Name _____

Hannah hears

hungry hippo

Write the sentence.

Name _____

Hannah hears a hungry hippo.

Ii

Practice by tracing the letter.
Then write the letter.

Practice by tracing the words.
Then write the words.

Name _____

inchworm

iguana

igloo

Indiana

Ii

Name _____

Inchworms itch

in Indiana

Write the sentence.

Name _____

Inchworms itch in Indiana.

Jj

Practice by tracing the letter.
Then write the letter.

Name _____

Practice by tracing the words.
Then write the words.

Name _____

jaguar

jump

jam

June

Write the phrase.

Name _____

Jumping jaguars

jolly jokes

Jumping jaguars tell jolly jokes.

Kk

Practice by tracing the letter.
Then write the letter.

Name _____

K K K K K

K K K K K K

Practice by tracing the words.
Then write the words.

Name _____

kangaroo

kite

key

Kelsey

Write the phrase.

Name _____

Kind Kelsey

keeps kangaroos

Write the sentence. Name _____

Kind Kelsey keeps kangaroos.

Practice by tracing the letter.
Then write the letter.

Name _____

Practice by tracing the words.
Then write the words.

Name _____

lion

lollipop

lick

Lori

Ll

Name _____

Little Lori

likes lions

Write the sentence.

Name _____

Little Lori likes lions and lollipops.

Mm

Practice by tracing the letter.
Then write the letter.

M M M M M M

m m m m m m m

Practice by tracing the words.
Then write the words.

Name _____

monkey

mushroom

moon

Megan

Write the phrase.

Name _____

Mommy monkeys

Megan's mushrooms

Write the sentence.

Name _____

Mommy monkeys mash Megan's mushrooms.

Nn

Practice by tracing the letter.
Then write the letter.

Name _____

N N N N N N N N N

n n n n n n n n

Practice by tracing the words.
Then write the words.

Name _____

newt

nest

note

Nebraska

Write the phrase.

Name _____

Nine newts

no nest

Write the sentence. Name _____

Nine newts have no nest.

Oo

Practice by tracing the letter.
Then write the letter.

Oo

Practice by tracing the words.
Then write the words.

Name _____

ostrich

octopus

olive

Olivia

Oo

Name _____

Olivia owns

one ostrich

Write the sentence. Name _____

Olivia owns one ostrich and one octopus.

Pp

Practice by tracing the letter.
Then write the letter.

P   P   P   P   P   P   P   P

p   p   p   p   p   p   p   p

Practice by tracing the words.
Then write the words.

Name _____

penguin

pizza

pencil

puppy

Pp

Pp

Write the phrase.

Name _____

puppy plays

pretty pool

Write the sentence. Name _____

The puppy plays in the pretty pool.

Practice by tracing the letter.
Then write the letter.

Name _____

Practice by tracing the words.
Then write the words.

Name _____

quail

queen

quarter

quit

Write the phrase.

Name _____

quiet queen

quits quarreling

Write the sentence.

Name _____

The quiet queen quits quarreling.

Rr

Practice by tracing the letter.
Then write the letter.

Name _____

R R R R R R R R R R

r r r r r r r r

Practice by tracing the words.
Then write the words.

Name _____

rabbit

ribbon

race

runs

Rr

Name _____

rabbits run

road race

Write the sentence.

Name _____

Rowdy rabbits run a road race.

Practice by tracing the letter.
Then write the letter.

Name _____

S   S   S   S   S   S   S

S   S   S   S   S   S   S

Practice by tracing the words.
Then write the words.

Name _____

seal

sun

shell

seven

Write the phrase.

Name _____

Seven shells

soft sunshine

Write the sentence.

Name _____

Seven shells shine in the soft

sunshine.

Tt

Practice by tracing the letter.
Then write the letter.

Practice by tracing the words.
Then write the words.

Name _____

turtle

tiger

tie

teach

Write the phrase.

Name _____

Ten turtles

teach tigers

Write the sentence.

Name _____

Tt

Ten turtles teach tigers.

Uu

Practice by tracing the letter.
Then write the letter.

Name _____

Practice by tracing the words.
Then write the words.

Name _____

umpire

umbrella

under

unhappy

Write the phrase.

Name _____

Unhappy umpires

ugly umbrellas

Write the sentence. Name _____

Unhappy umpires use ugly umbrellas.

Vv

Practice by tracing the letter.
Then write the letter.

Name _____

Practice by tracing the words.
Then write the words.

Name _____

vulture

violin

vest

van

Vv

Write the phrase.

Name _____

Vultures in vests

play violins

Write the sentence. Name _____

Vultures in vests play violins.

Ww

Practice by tracing the letter.
Then write the letter.

W W W W W W WW W

W W W W W W W

Ww

Practice by tracing the words.
Then write the words.

Name _____

whale

walrus

water

wishes

Ww

Write the phrase.

Name _____

walrus wishes

warm water

Ww

A walrus wishes for warm

water.

Practice by tracing the letter.
Then write the letter.

Name _____

Practice by tracing the words.
Then write the words.

Name _____

X-ray

Xylophone

Max

Extra

Write the phrase.

Name _____

extra saxophone

extra xylophone

Write the sentence. Name _____

Max got extra xylophones and saxophones.

Practice by tracing the letter.
Then write the letter.

Name _____

Yy

Practice by tracing the words.
Then write the words.

Name _____

yak

yo-yo

yarn

Your

Yy

Name _____

Your yak

Yellow yo-yo

Write the sentence. Name _____

Your yak plays with a

yellow yo-yo.

Zz

Practice by tracing the letter.
Then write the letter.

Name _____

Practice by tracing the words.
Then write the words.

Name _____

zebra

zipper

zoo

zigzag

Zz

Name _____

zany zebras

zigzag zoo

Write the sentence.

Name _____

Zany zebras zigzag through the zoo.

Numbers

Practice by tracing the words and numbers. Then write the words and numbers.

Name _____

one 1

two 2

three 3

four 4

five 5

Practice by tracing the words and numbers. Then write the words and numbers.

Name _____

six 6

seven 7

eight 8

nine 9

ten 10

Numbers

Practice by tracing the words and numbers. Then write the words and numbers.

Name _____

eleven 11

twelve 12

thirteen 13

fourteen 14

fifteen 15

Practice by tracing the words and numbers. Then write the words and numbers.

Name _____

sixteen 16

seventeen 17

eighteen 18

nineteen 19

twenty 20

Complete these sentences:

Name _____

I have _____ people in my family.

I have _____ students in my classroom.

I go to school at ____ o'clock.

For an after-school snack, I eat _____ grapes.

Practice by tracing the words.
Then write the words.

Name _____

square

circle

rectangle

oval

Color Words

Practice by tracing the words.
Then write the words.

Name _____

red

blue

yellow

orange

Practice by tracing the words.
Then write the words.

Name _____

black

white

purple

pink

Color Words

Practice by tracing the words.
Then write the words.

Name _____

brown

gray

green

Complete this sentence:

My favorite color

is _____ .

Practice by tracing the words and abbreviations. Then write the words and abbreviations.

Name _____

Sunday

Sun.

Monday

Mon.

Days of the Week
and Abbreviations

Practice by tracing the words and abbreviations. Then write the words and abbreviations.

Name _____

Tuesday

Tues.

Wednesday

Wed.

Practice by tracing the words and abbreviations. Then write the words and abbreviations.

Name _____

Thursday

Thurs.

Friday

Fri.

Practice by tracing the words and abbreviations. Then write the words and abbreviations.

Name _____

Saturday

Sat.

Today

Days of the Week and Abbreviations

Complete these sentences:

Name _____

Today is _____.

My birthday is _____.

The 100th day of school is _____.

The Fourth of July is celebrated on _____.

127

Practice by tracing the words and abbreviations. Then write the words and abbreviations.

Name _____

January

Jan.

February

Feb.

Practice by tracing the words and abbreviations. Then write the words and abbreviations.

Name _____

March

Mar.

April

Apr.

Months of the Year
and Abbreviations

Practice by tracing the words and abbreviations. Then write the words and abbreviations.

Name _____

May

June

July

August

Aug.

Practice by tracing the words and abbreviations. Then write the words and abbreviations.

Name _____

September

Sept.

October

Oct.

Practice by tracing the words and abbreviations. Then write the words and abbreviations.

Name _____

November

Nov.

December

Dec.

Practice by tracing the words.
Then write the words.

Name _____

winter

spring

summer

fall

Weather Words

Practice by tracing the words.
Then write the words.

Name _____

snow

rain

sunshine

sleet

Complete this sentence:

Outside I see _____.

Complete these sentences:

Name _____

Snow falls in _____.

Flowers bloom in _____.

In the _____,
we go swimming.

In the _____, leaves fall.

Practice by tracing the words.
Then write the words.

Name _____

Halloween

Easter

Fourth of July

Hanukkah

Practice by tracing the words.
Then write the words.

Name _____

Christmas

Thanksgiving

Kwanza

Happy Birthday

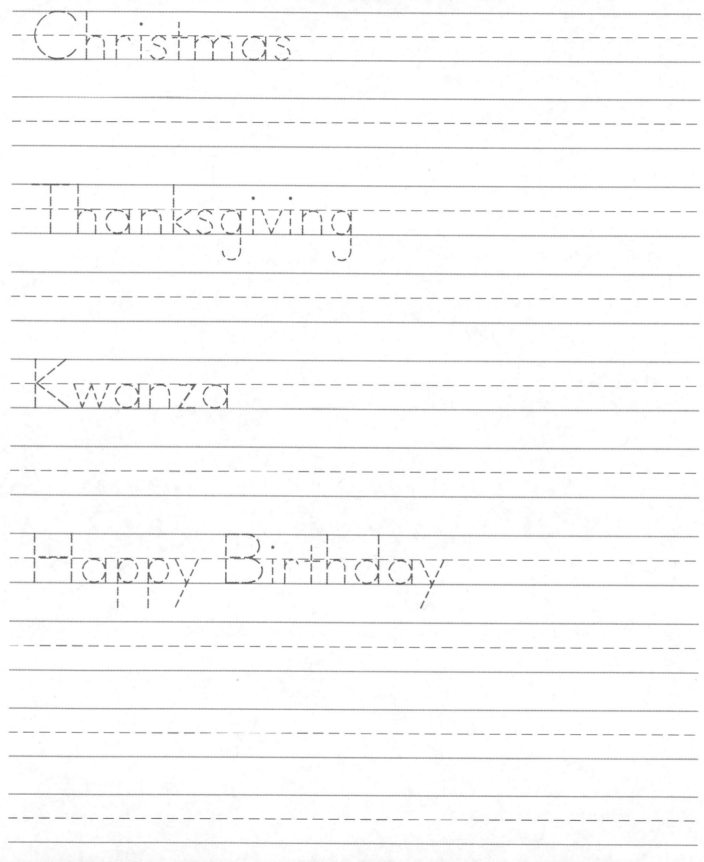

Practice by tracing the words.
Then write the words.

Name _____

gym

playground

classroom

principal's office

Practice by tracing the words.
Then write the words.

Name

math

music

art

gym

Practice by tracing the words.
Then write the words.

Name _____

science

spelling

social studies

writing

Practice by tracing the words.
Then write the words.

Name _____

teacher

aide

nurse

principal

Complete these sentences:

Name _____

My teacher's name is

_____ .

My school is called

_____ .

My classroom is _____ .

Complete these sentences:

Name _____

My principal's name is

_____ .

My favorite subject is

_____ .

I am in grade _____ .

Practice by tracing the words.
Then write the words.

Name _____

pencil

book

folder

paper

Practice by tracing the words.
Then write the words.

Name _____

awesome

excellent

way to go

great

Safety Words

Practice by tracing the words.
Then write the words.

Name _____

stop

go

caution

Complete these sentences: Name _____

A _____ light means go.

A _____ light means stop.

A _____ light means

caution.

Practice by tracing the words.
Then write the words.

Name _____

Mother

Father

Mom

Practice by tracing the words.
Then write the words.

Name _____

Dad

Grandma

Grandpa

Family Words

Practice by tracing the words.
Then write the words.

Name _____

aunt

uncle

brother

sister

Write the names of the people in your family.

Name _____

Neighborhood Words

Practice by tracing the words.
Then write the words.

Name _____

street

road

store

theater

Practice by tracing the words.
Then write the words.

Name _____

apartment

library

office

park

Complete these sentences:

Name _____

I live in a _____.

My address is _____

Write a sentence about your neighborhood:

_____

_____

_____

_____

_____

Practice by tracing the words.
Then write the words.

Name _____

country

city

state

town

Complete these sentences:

Name _____

My country is _____

_____.

My state is _____

_____.

My town is _____

_____.

Practice by tracing the words.
Then write the words.

Name _____

bread

meat

vegetable

fruit

Food Words

Practice by tracing the words.
Then write the words.

Name _____

soup

sandwich

cake

ice cream

Complete these sentences:

Name _____

My favorite foods are:

If I had a restaurant,

this would be my menu:

Practice by tracing the words.
Then write the words.

Name _____

right

left

up

down

Practice by tracing the words.
Then write the words.

Name _____

over

under

beside

behind

Practice by tracing the words.
Then write the words.

Name _____

soccer

football

baseball

golf

Practice by tracing the words.
Then write the words.

Name _____

basketball

swimming

volleyball

karate

Sports Words

Practice by tracing the words.
Then write the words.

Name _____

goal

point

team

run

Practice by tracing the words.
Then write the words.

Name _____

coach

score

guard

Complete this sentence:

My favorite sport is

●

Money Words

Practice by tracing the words.
Then write the words.

Name _____

dollar $

cents ¢

penny 1¢

Practice by tracing the words.
Then write the words.

Name _____

nickel 5¢

dime 10¢

quarter 25¢

Money Words

Write the correct word under the correct coin.

_____
- - - - - - - - - - - - - - - -
_____

_____
- - - - - - - - - - - - - - - -
_____

_____
- - - - - - - - - - - - - - - -
_____

_____
- - - - - - - - - - - - - - - -
_____

_____
- - - - - - - - - - - - - - - -
_____

_____
- - - - - - - - - - - - - - - -
_____

_____
- - - - - - - - - - - - - - - -
_____

_____
- - - - - - - - - - - - - - - -
_____

Practice by tracing the words.
Then write the words.

Name _____

run

swim

jump

fly

Action Words

Practice by tracing the words.
Then write the words.

Name _____

sing

read

play

study

Practice by tracing the words.
Then write the words.

Name _____

big

long

tall

good

Comparison Adjectives

Write the correct adjective next to the picture.

tall

taller

tallest

_____

_____

_____

Write the correct adjective next to the picture.

Name _____

big

bigger

biggest

_____

_____

_____

_____

_____

_____

Comparison Adjectives

Write the correct adjective next to the picture.

Name _____

small

smaller

smallest

_____

_____

_____

Write the correct adjective next to the picture.

Name _____

long

longer

longest

Write the correct adjective
next to the picture.

Name _____

good

better

best

_____

_____

_____

Write the correct comparative
adjective in the blank.

Name _____

I had the _____ time ever.
(good)

David is _____ than
(tall)
Susan.

It was the _____
(small)
kitten I had ever seen.

I ate the _____
(big)
ice cream sundae.

"Writing a Letter" Words

Practice by tracing the words.
Then write the words.

Name _____

Dear

Thank you

Sincerely

Your friend

Practice writing a thank-you note.

Name _____

Friendly Letter

Practice writing a letter.

Name _____

Practice addressing an envelope. Name _____

Aa

Practice by tracing the letter.
Then write the letter.

Name _____

Practice by tracing the words.
Then write the words.

Name _____

an

and

animals

April

Aa

Write the phrase.

Name _____

Arctic animals

act amusingly

Write the sentence.

Name _____

Arctic animals act amusingly.

Practice by tracing the letter.
Then write the letter.

Name _____

Practice by tracing the words.
Then write the words.

Name _____

big

boy

babble

baboon

Bb

Write the phrase.

Name _____

Big baboons

break balloons

Write the sentence.

Name _____

Big baboons break balloons.

Cc

Practice by tracing the letter.
Then write the letter.

Name _____

C C C C C

C C C C C

Practice by tracing the words.
Then write the words.

Name _____

can

candy

cool

count

Write the phrase.

Name _____

Cool crocodiles

count coconuts

Write the sentence.

Name _____

Cool crocodiles count coconuts.

Practice by tracing the letter.
Then write the letter.

Name _____

$\mathcal{D}$ $\mathcal{D}$ $\mathcal{D}$ $\mathcal{D}$ $\mathcal{D}$

d d d d d

Practice by tracing the words.
Then write the words.

Name _____

do

dog

dandelions

donuts

Dd

Write the phrase.

Dogs deliver

dandelions and
donuts

Write the sentence.

Dogs deliver dandelions and donuts.

Ee

Practice by tracing the letter.
Then write the letter.

Name _____

Practice by tracing the words.
Then write the words.

Name _____

each

eat

eels

eighty

Ee

Write the phrase.

Name _____

Electric eels

eat excitedly

Write the sentence.

Name _____

Electric eels eat excitedly.

Practice by tracing the letter.
Then write the letter.

Name _____

$\mathcal{F}$ $\mathcal{F}$ $\mathcal{F}$ $\mathcal{F}$ $\mathcal{F}$

f f f f f

Practice by tracing the words.
Then write the words.

Name _____

far

fat

fluff

feast

Ff

203

Write the phrase.

Name _____

Flamingos fluff

fancy feathers

Write the sentence.

Name _____

Flamingos fluff fancy feathers.

Gg

Practice by tracing the letter.
Then write the letter.

Name _____

Practice by tracing the words.
Then write the words.

Name _____

gag

gift

good

giggle

Gg

Write the phrase.

Giggling gophers

gag gifts

Write the sentence.

Name _____

Giggling gophers give gag gifts.

Hh

Practice by tracing the letter.
Then write the letter.

Name _____

Practice by tracing the words.
Then write the words.

Name _____

his

happy

he

hello

Write the phrase.

Name _____

Happy hippos

hang hammocks

Write the sentence.

Name _____

Happy hippos hang in their hammocks.

Ii

Practice by tracing the letter.
Then write the letter.

Name _____

Practice by tracing the words.
Then write the words.

Name _____

if

in

idea

itch

Ii

Write the phrase.

Name _____

Insects itch

in infield

Write the sentence.

Insects itch in the infield.

Practice by tracing the letter.
Then write the letter.

Name _____

Practice by tracing the words.
Then write the words.

Name _____

jam

job

jazz

junk

Write the phrase.

Name _____

juggling jaguars

to jazz

Write the sentence.

Name _____

Juggling jaguars jam to jazz.

Kk

Practice by tracing the letter.
Then write the letter.

Name _____

$\mathcal{K}$ $\mathcal{K}$ $\mathcal{K}$ $\mathcal{K}$ $\mathcal{K}$

$\mathcal{k}$ $\mathcal{k}$ $\mathcal{k}$ $\mathcal{k}$ $\mathcal{k}$

Practice by tracing the words.
Then write the words.

Name _____

kid

key

Kick

keep

Kk

Name _____

Kooky kangaroos

kick karate

Write the sentence.

Name _____

Kooky kangaroos kick in karate.

Ll

Practice by tracing the letter.
Then write the letter.

Name _____

$\mathscr{L}$ $\quad$ $\mathscr{L}$ $\quad$ $\mathscr{L}$ $\quad$ $\mathscr{L}$ $\quad$ $\mathscr{L}$ $\quad$ $\mathscr{L}$

ℓ $\quad$ ℓ $\quad$ ℓ $\quad$ ℓ $\quad$ ℓ

Practice by tracing the words.
Then write the words.

Name _____

low

land

lamb

little

Write the phrase.

Name _____

Little lambs

lemon lollipops

Write the sentence.

Name _____

Little lambs lick lemon lollipops.

Mm

Practice by tracing the letter.
Then write the letter.

Name _____

m m m m m

m m m m m

Practice by tracing the words.
Then write the words.

Name _____

mad

milk

monkeys

merry

Mm

Merry monkeys

make marmalade

Write the sentence.

Name _____

Merry monkeys make marmalade.

Practice by tracing the letter.
Then write the letter.

Name _____

n   n   n   n   n

m   m   m   m   m

Practice by tracing the words.
Then write the words.

Name _____

nap

name

near

night

Nn

Name _____

naughty gnats

never nap

Write the sentence.

Naughty gnats
never nap at
night.

Practice by tracing the letter.
Then write the letter.

Name _____

Practice by tracing the words.
Then write the words.

Name _____

out

often

once

order

Write the phrase.

Name _____

Ostriches often

onion omelettes

Write the sentence.

Name _____

Ostriches often
order onion
omelettes.

Pp

Practice by tracing the letter.
Then write the letter.

Name _____

Practice by tracing the words.
Then write the words.

Name _____

pan

pet

pick

paper

Write the phrase.

Name _____

Pandas paint

pictures paper

Write the sentence.

Name _____

Pandas paint pictures on paper.

Practice by tracing the letter.
Then write the letter.

Name _____

Q Q Q Q Q

q q q q q

Practice by tracing the words.
Then write the words.

Name _____

quit

quick

quart

quiet

Quick quails

unique quarter

Write the sentence.

Name _____

Quick quails quarrel over a unique quarter.

Rr

Practice by tracing the letter.
Then write the letter.

Name _____

R R R R R

N N N N N

Practice by tracing the words.
Then write the words.

Name _____

rat

run

rear

road

Rr

Name _____

Raccoons run

red cars

Write the sentence.

Name _____

Raccoons run races in red cars.

Ss

Practice by tracing the letter.
Then write the letter.

Name _____

Practice by tracing the words.
Then write the words.

Name _____

see

sing

stand

stow

Ss

Write the phrase.

Standing storks

sing swans

Write the sentence.

Name _____

Standing storks

sing with swans.

Practice by tracing the letter.
Then write the letter.

Name _____

Tt

Practice by tracing the words.
Then write the words.

Name _____

the

tip

told

twist

259

Write the phrase.

Name _____

Two tigers

tickle toes

Write the sentence.

Name _____

Two tigers tickle each other's toes.

Uu

Practice by tracing the letter.
Then write the letter.

𝓤 𝓤 𝓤 𝓤 𝓤

𝓾𝓾 𝓾𝓾 𝓾𝓾 𝓾𝓾 𝓾𝓾

Practice by tracing the words.
Then write the words.

Name _____

use

under

until

unhappy

Uu

Write the phrase.

Unicorns use

umbrellas under

Write the sentence.

Name _____

Unicorns use umbrellas under thunder.

Vv

Practice by tracing the letter.
Then write the letter.

Name _____

V   V   V   V   V   V

N   N   N   N   N

Practice by tracing the words.
Then write the words.

Name _____

very

vote

vine

vest

Vv

Name _____

Vultures vacuum

velvet vests

Write the sentence.

Name _____

Vultures vacuum in velvet vests.

Ww

Practice by tracing the letter.
Then write the letter.

Name _____

$\mathcal{W}$ $\mathcal{W}$ $\mathcal{W}$ $\mathcal{W}$ $\mathcal{W}$

w w w w w

Practice by tracing the words.
Then write the words.

Name _____

wet

west

wall

winter

Ww

Name _____

Wet walruses

to win

Write the sentence.

Name

Wet walruses
bowl to win.

Xx

Practice by tracing the letter.
Then write the letter.

Name _____

$\mathcal{X}$ $\mathcal{X}$ $\mathcal{X}$ $\mathcal{X}$ $\mathcal{X}$

$\mathcal{x}$ $\mathcal{x}$ $\mathcal{x}$ $\mathcal{x}$ $\mathcal{x}$

Practice by tracing the words.
Then write the words.

Name _____

x-ray

box

extra

xylophone

X-RAY MACHINE

FOX IN BOX

Xx

Name _____

x-ray boxes

with foxes

Write the sentence.

Name _____

Xandra x-rays

boxes with foxes.

X-RAY MACHINE

FOX IN BOX

Yy

Practice by tracing the letter.
Then write the letter.

Y Y Y Y Y

y y y y y

Practice by tracing the words.
Then write the words.

Name _____

you

yard

year

yellow

Write the phrase.

Name _____

Yaks yell

Yodel loudly

Write the sentence.

Name _____

Yaks yell and yodel loudly.

Practice by tracing the letter.
Then write the letter.

Name _____

Practice by tracing the words.
Then write the words.

Name _____

zero

zoom

zone

zipper

Write the phrase.

Name _____

zigzagging zebras

zip zoom

Write the sentence.

Name _____

Zigzagging zebras zip and zoom.

Numbers

Practice by tracing the words and numbers. Then write the words and numbers.

Name _____

one 1

two 2

three 3

four 4

five 5

Practice by tracing the words and numbers. Then write the words and numbers.

Name _____

six 6

seven 7

eight 8

nine 9

ten 10

Practice by tracing the words and numbers. Then write the words and numbers.

Name _____

eleven 11

twelve 12

thirteen 13

fourteen 14

fifteen 15

Practice by tracing the words and numbers. Then write the words and numbers.

Name _____

sixteen 16

seventeen 17

eighteen 18

nineteen 19

twenty 20

Shape Words

Practice by tracing the words.
Then write the words.

Name _____

square

circle

rectangle

oval

Practice by tracing the words.
Then write the words.

Name _____

red

blue

yellow

orange

Color Words

Practice by tracing the words.
Then write the words.

Name _____

black

white

purple

pink

Practice by tracing the words.
Then write the words.

Name _____

brown

gray

green

Complete this sentence:

My favorite color

is _____.

Days of the Week
and Abbreviations

Practice by tracing the words and abbreviations. Then write the words and abbreviations.

Name _____

Sunday

Sun.

Monday

Mon.

Practice by tracing the words and abbreviations. Then write the words and abbreviations.

Name _____

Tuesday

Tues.

Wednesday

Wed.

Days of the Week
and Abbreviations

Practice by tracing the words and abbreviations. Then write the words and abbreviations.

Name _____

Thursday

Thurs.

Friday

Fri.

Practice by tracing the words and abbreviations. Then write the words and abbreviations.

Name _____

Saturday

Sat.

Today

Months of the Year
and Abbreviations

Practice by tracing the words and abbreviations. Then write the words and abbreviations.

Name _____

January

Jan.

February

Feb.

Practice by tracing the words and abbreviations. Then write the words and abbreviations.

Name _____

March

Mar.

April

Apr.

Months of the Year
and Abbreviations

Practice by tracing the words and abbreviations. Then write the words and abbreviations.

Name _____

May

June

July

August

Aug.

Practice by tracing the words and abbreviations. Then write the words and abbreviations.

Name _____

September

Sept.

October

Oct.

Months of the Year
and Abbreviations

Practice by tracing the words and abbreviations. Then write the words and abbreviations.

Name _____

November

Nov.

December

Dec.

Practice by tracing the words.
Then write the words.

Name _____

winter

spring

summer

fall

Weather Words

Practice by tracing the words.
Then write the words.

Name _____

snow

rain

sunshine

sleet

Complete this sentence:

Today we have

Practice by tracing the words.
Then write the words.

Name _____

Halloween

Easter

Fourth of July

Hanukkah

Practice by tracing the words.
Then write the words.

Name _____

Christmas

Thanksgiving

Kwanza

Happy Birthday

Practice by tracing the words.
Then write the words.

Name _____

gym

playground

classroom

principal's office

School Words

Practice by tracing the words.
Then write the words.

Name _____

math

music

art

gym

Practice by tracing the words.
Then write the words.

Name _____

science

spelling

social studies

writing

School Words

Practice by tracing the words.
Then write the words.

Name _____

teacher

aide

nurse

principal

Practice by tracing the words.
Then write the words.

Name _____

pencil

book

folder

paper

Safety Words

Practice by tracing the words.
Then write the words.

Name _____

stop

go

caution

Practice by tracing the words.
Then write the words.

Name _____

Mother

Father

Mom

Family Words

Practice by tracing the words.
Then write the words.

Name _____

Dad

Grandma

Grandpa

Practice by tracing the words.
Then write the words.

Name _____

aunt

uncle

brother

sister

Family Words

Write the names of the people
in your family.

Name _____

Practice by tracing the words.
Then write the words.

Name _____

street

road

store

theater

Neighborhood Words

Practice by tracing the words.
Then write the words.

apartment

library

office

park

Complete these sentences:

Name _____

I live in a

_____.

My address is

_____.

Write a sentence about your neighborhood:

Money Words

Practice by tracing the words.
Then write the words.

Name _____

dollar $

cents ¢

penny /¢

Practice by tracing the words.
Then write the words.

Name _____

nickel 5¢

dime 10¢

quarter 25¢

Money Words

Practice by tracing the words.
Then write the words.

_____

- - - - - - - - - - - - - - - -

_____

_____

- - - - - - - - - - - - - - - -

_____

_____

- - - - - - - - - - - - - - - -

_____

_____

- - - - - - - - - - - - - - - -

_____

_____

- - - - - - - - - - - - - - - -

_____

_____

- - - - - - - - - - - - - - - -

_____

_____

- - - - - - - - - - - - - - - -

_____

_____

- - - - - - - - - - - - - - - -

_____

Practice by tracing the words.
Then write the words.

Name _____

run

swim

jump

fly

Action Words

Practice by tracing the words.
Then write the words.

Name _____

sing

read

play

study

Adjectives

Practice by tracing the words.
Then write the words.

Name _____

big

long

tall

good

Comparison Adjectives

Write the correct adjective next to the picture.

Name _____

tall

taller

tallest

_____

_____

_____

Write the correct adjective next to the picture.

big

bigger

biggest

_____

_ _ _ _ _ _ _ _ _ _ _ _ _ _ _ _ _

_____

_ _ _ _ _ _ _ _ _ _ _ _ _ _ _ _ _

_____

_ _ _ _ _ _ _ _ _ _ _ _ _ _ _ _ _

Comparison Adjectives

Write the correct adjective
next to the picture.

Name _____

small

smaller

smallest

_____
- - - - - - - - - - - - - - - - -
_____

_____
- - - - - - - - - - - - - - - - -
_____

_____
- - - - - - - - - - - - - - - - -
_____

Write the correct adjective
next to the picture.

Name _____

long

longer

longest

Write the correct adjective
next to the picture.

Name _____

good

better

best

Write the correct comparative
adjective in the blank.

Name _____

I had the _____
(good)

time ever.

David is _____
(tall)

than Susan.

It was the

_____ *kitten*
(small)

I had ever seen.

I ate the _____
(big)

ice cream sundae.

Practice by tracing the words.
Then write the words.

Name _____

Dear

Thank you

Sincerely

Your friend

Practice writing a thank-you note.

Name _____

Friendly Letter

Practice writing a letter to your friend.

Name _____

Practice by tracing the words.
Then write the words.

Name _____

dictionary

definition

alphabetical order

Pronouns

Practice by tracing the words.
Then write the words.

Name _____

I

me

you

her

we

Practice by tracing the words.
Then write the words.

Name _____

he

she

they

them

Practice by tracing the words.
Then write the words.

Name _____

I'll

she'll

we'll

you'll

Practice by tracing the words.
Then write the words.

Name _____

sentence

paragraph

poem

story

Complete these sentences:

Name _____

At the end of a

_____, you

put a period.

A _____

has a main idea.

A _____ does not

have to rhyme.

A _____ has a

beginning, middle,

and end.

Practice by tracing the words.
Then write the words.

Name _____

fiction

nonfiction

biography

autobiography

A _____ book
tells about things
that really
happened.

A _____ book
tells a story
that is not real.

A _____
tells the story of
someone's life.

Practice by tracing the words.
Then write the words.

Name _____

add

subtract

multiply

divide

Math Words

Practice by tracing the words.
Then write the words.

Name _____

sum

product

regrouping

Complete this sentence:

When you add,

the answer is

called a _____.

Practice by tracing the words.
Then write the words.

Name _____

one-half

one-fourth

one-eighth

three-quarters

Use words from the previous page to complete these sentences:

Name _____

There is _____ glass of milk left. The pizza is _____ gone. There is only _____ of the pizza left.

Practice by tracing the words.
Then write the words.

Name _____

yard

inch

foot

mile

meter

There are three feet in a _____.
There are twelve _____ in a _____.
There are thirty-six inches in a _____.
There are 1760 yards in a _____.

Practice by tracing the words.
Then write the words.

Name _____

habitat

experiment

food chain

water cycle

Practice by tracing the words.
Then write the words.

Name _____

paint

draw

sketch

sculpture

Practice by tracing the words.
Then write the words.

Name _____

sing

piano

note

strings

Practice by tracing the words.
Then write the words.

Name _____

band

violin

drums

trumpet

Traditional Manuscript

Aa Bb Cc Dd Ee Ff Gg

Hh Ii Jj Kk Ll Mm Nn

Oo Pp Qq Rr Ss Tt Uu

Vv Ww Xx Yy Zz

0 1 2 3 4 5 6 7 8 9

Traditional Cursive

Aa Bb Cc Dd Ee Ff

Gg Hh Ii Jj Kk Ll

Mm Nn Oo Pp Qq

Rr Ss Tt Uu Vv Ww

Xx Yy Zz